Report of the United States of America
Submitted to the U.N. High Commissioner for Human Rights
In Conjunction with the Universal Periodic Review

I. Introduction

1.   As a nation founded on the human rights principles of equality under the law and respect for the dignity of the individual, the United States is firmly dedicated to the promotion of human rights.

2.   Human rights are embedded in our Constitution, laws, and policies at every level, and governmental action is subject to review by an independent judiciary and debated by a free press and an engaged civil society. Not only do individuals within the United States have effective legal means to seek policy, administrative, and judicial remedies for human rights violations and abuses, the government itself pursues extensive and comprehensive enforcement actions to create systematic reform. Our federal system enables our nation to test new methods and strategies for promoting human rights at the state and local levels. While recognizing that there is more work to be done, we are constantly striving to create a fairer and more just society, as reflected in the programs and policies discussed in this report.

II.   Methodology and Consultation Process

3.   In our first UPR in 2010, the United States supported in whole or in part 173 of 228 recommendations. We have divided these recommendations into ten thematic areas and have structured Section III of this report accordingly. Working groups comprising experts from relevant federal agencies addressed each of the thematic areas, meeting periodically, assessing progress on the recommendations, and consulting with civil society to share updates and receive feedback.

4.   This report responds to all recommendations that we supported in whole or in part, even where such recommendations fall outside the scope of the United States' human rights obligations and commitments.

III.   Progress and Challenges

A. Domestic Mechanisms for Human Rights Implementation

Reviewing domestic laws and institutions
Recommendations 65 and 74

5.   The United States is committed to effective implementation of our human rights treaty obligations and has multiple mechanisms that provide for regular review of our federal and state laws and policies. We have, in recent years, improved engagement with state and local governments to foster better awareness of human rights obligations at the state, tribal, and local levels. State and local government officials have been members of recent U.S. delegations presenting reports on the Convention on the Elimination of All Forms of Racial Discrimination, the Optional Protocols to the Convention on the Rights of the Child, the International Covenant on Civil and Political Rights, and the Convention Against Torture. The United States intends to

continue including state and local representatives, and we have invited them to several civil society consultations during this UPR cycle.

6.	In addition, we have reminded federal, state, local, tribal, and territorial officials of our human rights treaty obligations and notified them of upcoming treaty reporting. For example, in 2014, the State Department wrote to state, local, territorial, and tribal officials to inform them of our upcoming presentations and this UPR. Federal officials have conducted targeted training sessions on human rights treaties for state and local officials, such as an August 2014 conference of state- and local-level employment nondiscrimination agencies. We have worked regularly with relevant associations, such as the 160-member International Association of Official Human Rights Agencies and the National Association of Attorneys General, to provide their members with information on U.S. human rights treaty obligations and commitments and to discuss the role they can play.

7.	The United States has continued to receive and consider proposals for a national human rights institution. Although we do not have an NHRI, we have multiple protections and mechanisms to reinforce respect for human rights, including independent judiciaries at federal and state levels and numerous state, tribal, and local human rights institutions.

Human rights education, training, and engagement with civil society
Recommendations 87 and 225

8.	The United States continually works to improve human rights training for those in government. For instance, we held a 2014 roundtable on domestic violence, sexual assault, non-discrimination, and human rights to educate U.S. government participants about U.S. human rights obligations and commitments relevant to these issues, helping them identify and understand relevant human rights resources. Additionally, since 2012, we have convened interagency roundtable discussions on legal aid to explore ways in which civil legal aid can promote access to health services, housing, education, employment, family stability, and community well-being.

9.	We also have a number of regular training programs related to the promotion and protection of human rights. For example, law enforcement and immigration screening personnel receive training on prohibitions of unlawful discrimination and racial or ethnic profiling, and on protections for those fleeing persecution, human trafficking, and certain other crimes.

10.	Civil society plays a critical role in promoting human rights in the United States. Our laws and institutions create an enabling environment where civil society is encouraged to act freely without fear of reprisal. Consistent with our commitment to supporting free and robust civil society at home and around the world, we conduct frequent, in-depth consultations with civil society on issues related to our human rights record, including in preparation for this UPR (see Section II) and for treaty reports.

B. Civil Rights and Discrimination

Profiling and excessive use of force by law enforcement
Recommendations 68, 101, 150-151, 208-209, and 219

11.   The United States is dedicated to eliminating racial discrimination and the use of excessive force in policing. The vast majority of police officers in the United States are committed to respecting their fellow citizens' civil rights as they carry out difficult and dangerous work. But where there is individual or systemic officer misconduct, appropriate responses are required. In the past six years, the U.S. Department of Justice has opened more than 20 civil investigations into police departments that may be engaging in a pattern or practice of conduct that deprives persons of their rights. These investigations have focused on excessive force, discrimination, coercive sexual conduct, and unlawful stops, searches, and arrests. In the same time period, DOJ has reached 15 settlements with police departments.

12.   On December 4, 2014, DOJ announced that its civil rights investigation into the Cleveland, Ohio, Division of Police had found a pattern or practice of unreasonable and unnecessary use of force. Consequently, DOJ and the city of Cleveland have committed to develop a court-enforceable agreement that will include an independent monitor to oversee necessary reforms. DOJ has taken similar action in the past five years, making public findings of discriminatory policing and/or excessive force and working toward long-term solutions in 13 states and jurisdictions.

13.   In addition, in the last five years, DOJ has criminally prosecuted more than 335 individual police officers for misconduct, including use of excessive force, and obtained 254 convictions as of January 1, 2015.

14.   We are also working to strengthen police-community relations. For example, in Ferguson, Missouri, in addition to opening civil and criminal investigations after the August 2014 shooting of Michael Brown, DOJ sent mediators to create a dialogue between police, city officials, and residents to reduce tension in the community. In addition, DOJ is involved in a voluntary, independent, and objective assessment of the St. Louis County Police Department, looking at training, use of force, handling mass demonstrations, and other areas where reform may be needed.

15.   As President Obama has said, "[t]he fact is, in too many parts of this country, a deep distrust exists between law enforcement and communities of color." At the President's request, the Attorney General convened roundtable discussions among law enforcement, elected officials, and community members in six cities in December 2014 and January 2015. The President also appointed a Task Force on 21st Century Policing, which is examining how to strengthen public trust and foster strong relationships between local law enforcement and the communities they protect.

16.   In December 2014, DOJ announced an updated policy on profiling by federal law enforcement and state and local officers participating in federal law enforcement task forces. This policy instructs that law enforcement officers may not consider race, ethnicity, national

origin, gender, gender identity, religion, or sexual orientation to any degree when making routine or spontaneous law enforcement decisions, unless the characteristics apply to a suspect's description. The policy applies a uniform standard to all federal law enforcement, national security, and intelligence activities conducted by law enforcement components.

Racial bias in the criminal justice system and mandatory minimum sentences
Recommendations 96-97

17.   The United States is taking steps to address the disproportionate percentage of minorities, particularly African-Americans, in the criminal justice system. For example, the Fair Sentencing Act of 2010 has reduced the disparity between more lenient sentences for powder cocaine charges and more severe sentences for crack cocaine charges (the latter of which are more frequently brought against racial minorities). Data from the U.S. Sentencing Commission through June 2014 indicate that 7,706 federal crack offenders' sentences have been reduced as a result of retroactive application of this change: of these offenders, an estimated 90 percent are African-American.

18.   Lower penalty guidelines for all drug offenders went into effect in November 2014. The USSC estimates that these changes will reduce penalties by an average of 11 months for 70 percent of newly-sentenced drug trafficking offenders, and that more than 40,000 currently-imprisoned offenders may be eligible to have their sentences retroactively reduced by an average of 25 months.

19.   With the Smart on Crime Initiative, launched in 2013, the Attorney General directed all federal prosecutors to, inter alia, reserve stringent mandatory minimum narcotics charges and repeat offender charges for only the most serious offenders. This has contributed to less use of incarceration for less-serious drug offenses. DOJ is working with the U.S. Congress on legislation to reform mandatory minimum sentences and reduce their application to nonviolent offenders.

Discrimination based on religion and hate crimes
Recommendations 64, 98-99, 103, 106, 189, and 190-191

20.   The United States is committed to preventing and effectively prosecuting hate crimes. In 2009, we enacted a powerful new tool, the Shepard-Byrd Hate Crimes Prevention Act, which enhanced federal prosecution for violent crimes motivated by religious, racial, or national origin bias and enabled federal prosecution of crimes based on sexual orientation, gender, gender identity, and disability. Over the last five years, DOJ has obtained convictions of more than 160 defendants on such charges, a nearly 50 percent increase over the previous five years. DOJ also continues to prosecute other hate crimes, and in 2014 assisted Kansas authorities in the investigation of a fatal shooting at a Kansas City Jewish community center. In January 2015, the FBI began collecting more detailed data on bias-motivated crimes, including those committed against Arab, Hindu, and Sikh individuals.

21.   We continue to actively fight all forms of religious discrimination. For instance, in recent years, DOJ has received a large number of complaints involving members of Muslim communities alleging unfair obstacles to building or expanding places of worship. Ten of the 34 DOJ investigations in this area since 2010, and five of the six lawsuits, have involved mosques or Islamic schools. In one such case, DOJ filed an amicus brief in a state court and initiated a federal lawsuit to ensure that a mosque would be permitted to open and operate in Murfreesboro, Tennessee.

22.   In 2013, DOJ successfully resolved two complaints alleging that Sikh individuals were denied access to county court systems because of their religious headwear. Those counties subsequently adopted policies that prohibit discrimination because of religious head coverings.

23.   We continue our robust efforts to eliminate religious discrimination in employment: the U.S. Equal Employment Opportunity Commission is currently litigating a suit before the U.S. Supreme Court against an employer for refusing to hire a Muslim worker out of concern that she would request religious accommodation to wear a headscarf.

24.   We also continue to seek input from affected communities on these issues. Federal prosecutors have been directly involved in outreach to members of Arab, Muslim, and Sikh communities, working to strengthen trust; to provide protection from hate crimes, bullying, and discrimination; and to make clear that the United States cannot conduct surveillance on any individual based solely on race, ethnicity, or religion. In addition, the U.S. Department of Homeland Security leads or participates in regular roundtable meetings among community leaders and federal, state, and local government officials to discuss the impact of its programs, policies, and procedures on members of diverse demographic groups, including religious minorities.

Racial discrimination in voting, employment, housing, education, and health
Recommendations 62, 67, 94, 100, 107, 109, and 116

25.   *Voting*—The right to vote is fundamental to democracy. Accordingly, ensuring equal access to the ballot box is critical, and the Voting Rights Act of 1965 remains our most powerful tool in this effort. Although the U.S. Supreme Court invalidated a key part of that law, which required prior federal review of changes to certain jurisdictions' voting practices, DOJ has recently filed three challenges to discriminatory practices in Texas and North Carolina asking that those states be required to clear future voting changes with DOJ or a federal court. In October 2014, a federal court found Texas' new voter identification law to be intentionally discriminatory against members of minority groups. DOJ has also vigorously enforced the voting rights of those belonging to language-minority groups, bringing or participating in cases to protect persons with limited English proficiency.

26.   *Labor and Employment*—We are committed to protecting all individuals, including members of racial minorities, from workplace discrimination. From 2011-2013, EEOC received 293,086 individual complaints of discrimination, resolved 320,890 charges, and recovered a total of $1.1 billion for affected employees through the administrative process. Over this three-year

period, EEOC filed 603 lawsuits on behalf of individuals subjected to workplace discrimination, resolved 817 such lawsuits, and recovered an additional $173.8 million for affected workers. In 2013, DOJ collected record civil penalties from employers in resolving employment discrimination claims based on citizenship status or national origin, and in 2014, it secured a record amount of back pay for these discrimination victims.

27. These robust enforcement efforts have produced tangible systemic results as well. For example, in 2014, in a case involving the hiring practices of the New York City Fire Department, DOJ obtained its largest-ever settlement in an employment discrimination case, resulting in jobs for some 290 eligible claimants and $98 million in monetary damages. In the last fiscal year, the Department of Labor recovered nearly 1,800 job offers and over $12 million in financial remedies for 23,000 workers for claims of racial and other forms of discrimination involving federal contractors.

28. *Housing*—We have aggressively pursued remedies for racial discrimination in housing and improved legal protections and policies to prevent such discrimination. Our Department of Housing and Urban Development is working to strengthen the housing market to bolster the economy and protect consumers, meet the need for quality affordable homes, utilize housing as a platform for improving quality of life, and build inclusive and sustainable communities free from discrimination. For example, in 2013, HUD published a proposed regulation to clarify program participants' obligation to take proactive steps to overcome historic patterns of segregation, promote fair housing choice, and foster inclusive communities. Under the proposed rule, HUD will collect data on patterns of integration and segregation to better identify potential fair housing issues.

29. The United States also aggressively enforces fair lending laws against lenders engaging in discriminatory practices. We have brought legal action to remedy such abuses and established a Financial Fraud Enforcement Task Force with state and local partners to proactively investigate these practices. Since 2010, DOJ has filed or resolved 26 lending matters. The resulting settlements have provided for over $900 million in monetary relief, including a $335 million settlement with Countrywide Financial and a $234.3 million settlement with Wells Fargo for racial and ethnic discrimination in mortgage loans; and a $98 million settlement with Ally Financial Inc. and Ally Bank for racial and ethnic discrimination in auto loans.

30. *Education*—We seek to ensure equal educational opportunities for all students by enforcing laws that prohibit discrimination in education, including on the basis of race, color, and national origin. For example, in 2011, the U.S. government reached a resolution with the Los Angeles Unified School District in California, the second-largest public school district in the United States, to develop and implement a comprehensive plan to eliminate the disproportionate discipline of African-American students and others. Since then, the suspension rate in that school district has fallen significantly, including a more than 50 percent decrease for African-American students.

31. Similarly, as a result of agreements, school districts in Kentucky and Delaware are working to eliminate the disproportionate discipline of African-American students and others, including by reviewing and revising discipline policies and improving collection of student-

discipline data. In 2014, we issued guidance to assist schools in administering discipline without discriminating on the basis of race, color, or national origin. In addition, DOJ monitors and seeks further relief as necessary in approximately 180 school districts that have a history of segregation and remain under court supervision.

32.   We also have numerous laws allowing individuals to sue schools, school districts, or institutions of higher education to remedy individual cases of discrimination, beyond the systemic remedies pursued by the federal government. See Paragraphs 103-104 for more on education.

33.   *Health*—We are committed to eliminating health disparities and promoting health, and we actively enforce federal civil rights laws to help ensure that all people have equal access to health care and social service programs. In 2011, the Department of Health and Human Services launched the United States' first plan to specifically address persistent racial and ethnic health disparities. By law, all persons in the United States, including persons without valid immigration status, are entitled to emergency health services.

34.   For example, after securing a settlement in 2010, HHS monitored the University of Pittsburgh Medical Center for three years to ensure that closure of a hospital in a predominantly African-American community did not have a disparate impact on residents' access to healthcare. Additionally, HHS piloted a multi-state project to support hospitals in providing language access services to limited-English proficient populations in rural communities. During 2012-2013, HHS conducted compliance reviews of 45 such hospitals' language access programs. See Paragraphs 100-101 for more on health.

Discrimination against lesbian, gay, bisexual, and transgender individuals
Recommendations 86 and 112

35.   Equal protection of the rights of LGBT individuals is critically important to the United States, and we have made extraordinary strides to overcome obstacles and institutional biases that too often affect these individuals.

36.   In a landmark 2013 ruling, *United States v. Windsor*, the U.S. Supreme Court struck down the federal government's ban on recognizing same-sex marriages. Since then, we have worked to implement that decision by treating married same-sex couples the same as married opposite-sex couples with respect to the relevant benefits and obligations, to the greatest extent possible under the law. As a result, married same-sex couples are now eligible for many federal benefits and recognition, including in the areas of taxation, immigration, student financial aid, and military and veterans' benefits. As of January 2015, same-sex couples can marry in 36 of our 50 states and the District of Columbia.

37.   In the area of education, we have resolved a number of cases involving harassment of LGBT individuals in public schools. For example, in 2013, the U.S. government entered into a first-of-its-kind settlement agreement with the Arcadia Unified School District in California to resolve allegations of discrimination against a transgender student. In 2014, the U.S. Department of Education released guidance describing the responsibilities of colleges,

universities, and public schools to address sexual violence and other forms of sex discrimination, including discrimination based on gender identity.

38. In the area of policing, in 2014, DOJ's Community Relations Service launched transgender training for law enforcement officials that helps improve officer understanding and community relations.

39. In the area of employment, President Obama signed an order prohibiting federal contractors from discriminating against applicants and employees on the basis of sexual orientation or gender identity and adding gender identity as a prohibited basis for discrimination in federal employment. Furthermore, the U.S. government has taken the position that federal law prohibiting sex discrimination in employment extends to discrimination based on gender identity, including transgender status, and that LGBT workers stigmatized for failing to meet sex-based stereotypes may also pursue discrimination claims. In 2011, President Obama also announced the final repeal of the "Don't Ask, Don't Tell" law that barred gay men and lesbians from serving openly in the military.

Discrimination against persons with disabilities
Recommendations 114 and 198

40. The United States has robust protections to prevent discrimination against persons with disabilities and has actively enforced these protections since our last report. In 2009, we launched an aggressive effort to eliminate unnecessary segregation of persons with disabilities, helping protect the rights of more than 46,000 individuals, including through groundbreaking agreements with six U.S. states. In 2013 alone, we participated in 18 such enforcement matters around the country.

41. The United States vigilantly protects the workplace rights of persons with disabilities. For example, in 2013, the EEOC obtained the largest jury verdict in its history ($240 million) on behalf of workers with intellectual disabilities who were subjected to verbal and physical abuse and poor living conditions by their employer. While the verdict was later reduced to comply with statutory limits, it restored the dignity of the workers and brought public attention to the treatment of persons with intellectual disabilities in U.S. workplaces. New regulations have also strengthened accountability for federal contractors' efforts to recruit persons with disabilities and protections for the equal employment rights of veterans, including disabled veterans.

42. The United States funds a network of independent agencies in all states and territories to protect the rights of people with disabilities and their families through legal representation, advocacy, referral, and education. These agencies are the largest providers of legally-based advocacy services to people with disabilities in the United States.

C. Criminal Justice

Prisons
Recommendations 70, 145, 152, 162, 163, 174, 177-179, and 186

43.   The United States continues to strive to improve living conditions throughout its confinement facilities. To that end, we ensure that all offenders housed in federal custody have access to medical care on-site, and in the community if needed.

44.   In 2012, we issued regulations implementing the Prison Rape Elimination Act to prevent, detect, and respond to sexual abuse in federal, state, and local confinement facilities. These regulations include greater protections for juvenile offenders in adult facilities; new restrictions on cross-gender observation and searches; minimum staffing ratios in juvenile facilities; expanded medical and mental health care, including reproductive health care, for victims of prison rape; greater protections for LGBT and gender non-conforming inmates; and independent audits of all covered facilities.

45.   States must certify that all facilities under their operational control, including facilities run by private entities on behalf of the state, fully comply with these regulations; if they do not, they lose certain federal funding unless they pledge to devote that funding to compliance. Six states and one U.S. territory have been subjected to a five percent reduction in federal funding after declining to provide an assurance or certification of compliance.

46.   In December 2014, we issued guidance to states and local agencies to strengthen the quality of education services provided to youth in confinement. It includes principles for improving education practices and addresses the educational and civil rights requirements applicable to confined youth, including those with disabilities.

47.   We are committed to providing formerly incarcerated people with fair opportunities to rejoin their communities and become productive, law-abiding citizens. To this end, the Attorney General has called upon elected officials across the country to enact reforms to restore the voting rights of all who have served their terms in prison or jail, completed their parole or probation, and paid their fines.

48.   The U.S. Constitution guarantees to individuals the right to petition a federal court for a writ of habeas corpus, and we provide state and federal prisoners, including those sentenced to capital punishment, a well-defined means to raise post-conviction claims in federal court if their constitutional rights were violated in lower courts. Habeas review in federal courts is an important vehicle for protecting the constitutional rights of both state and federal inmates.

Capital punishment
Recommendations 95, 118, 134, and 135

49.   U.S. constitutional restraints, in addition to federal and state laws and practices, limit the use of capital punishment to the most serious offenses, such as murder, in the most aggravated

circumstances and with strict limitations. It is barred for any individual less than 18 years of age at the time of the crime and for individuals found by a court to have a significant intellectual disability. There are strict prohibitions against the use of any method of execution that would inflict cruel and unusual punishment and against imposition of the death penalty in a racially discriminatory manner. Federal and state laws require that sentencing decisions be individualized to the particular offender and offense. The President has directed DOJ to conduct a review of how the death penalty is being applied in the United States. Additionally, on January 23, the U.S. Supreme Court agreed to hear an argument, and is expected to rule in June 2015, on whether the lethal injection protocol used in executions by Oklahoma constitutes cruel and unusual punishment under the Eighth Amendment of our Constitution.

50.   When an individual may be subject to capital punishment, the appellate process is substantial and thorough, with ample opportunity to challenge a conviction and penalty through direct appeal and habeas review.   The Constitution requires that all criminal defendants, including capital defendants, receive effective assistance of counsel.

51.   The number of states that have the death penalty, the number of persons executed each year, and the size of the population on death row have continued to decline since our last report. Currently, federal law and laws in 32 U.S. states provide for capital punishment. Since our last UPR, three states have repealed their capital punishment laws: Illinois (2011), Connecticut (2012), and Maryland (2013). Only seven states carried out a total of 35 executions in 2014— the lowest number of executions in the United States since 1994. The federal government has carried out no executions since our last UPR; in fact, it has not executed an inmate since 2003 and only three since 1963.

Criminal justice and international issues
Recommendations 173 and 175

52.   Through DOJ's Human Rights and Special Prosecutions Section and other U.S. agency components, we investigate and prosecute human rights violators and other international criminals. Recently, we obtained convictions of two U.S. citizens for unlawfully procuring citizenship after they concealed their participation in a 1982 massacre of civilians in a Guatemalan village, and another on the same charges after she concealed her participation in killings during the 1994 Rwandan genocide.

53.   We also assess and carry out requests for international extradition in conformity with applicable extradition treaty provisions in force between the United States and the requesting state. We have extradited a number of persons accused of conduct constituting crimes such as genocide and war crimes, though such requests have been infrequent.

D. Indigenous Issues
Recommendations 83, 85, 199-203, 205, and 206

54.   The United States has made substantial advances to better protect the rights of indigenous peoples domestically. In December 2010, President Obama announced our support for the UN Declaration on the Rights of Indigenous Peoples, following review and three informal consultations with tribal governments, indigenous groups, and NGOs.

55.   We continue to engage in frequent and extensive domestic dialogues on matters of importance to indigenous peoples. In addition, we hold an annual White House Tribal Nations Conference with the leadership of tribal governments, where the President, the Vice President, many members of the Cabinet, dozens of senior U.S. officials, and hundreds of tribal leaders discuss issues such as tribal self-determination, including self-governance; healthcare; economic and infrastructure development; education; protection of land and natural resources; and other matters of priority to tribal governments. We also participated in the September 2014 World Conference on Indigenous Peoples, and were pleased that the four main priorities advocated by tribal government leaders were incorporated into the Outcome Document.

56.   In 2013, President Obama issued an order creating the White House Council on Native American Affairs consisting of the heads of various federal agencies to improve high-level coordination on the pressing issues facing tribal communities.

57.   In December 2014 we unveiled "Generation Indigenous," a major initiative to remove barriers to success for Native youth. It includes college and career readiness programs, leadership training, a listening tour by members of the President's cabinet to hear about the aspirations and concerns of Native youth, and a summit to discuss preservation of Native languages. The Department of the Interior, which educates 48,000 American Indian students across 23 states, issued a comprehensive reform plan in June 2014, and ED has proposed new education grants to better meet the needs of American Indian and Alaska Native students.

58.   We have further taken action to address discrimination against members of tribal communities and Native individuals. DOL enforces non-discrimination in employment for these groups by federal contractors. Since our last UPR, DOJ has enforced civil rights laws on behalf of American Indians and Alaska Natives in several areas, including protection of religious practices, education, voting, fair lending, corrections, access to courts by non-English speaking Native individuals, hate crimes, sex trafficking, and excessive use of force by police.

59.   Since 2010, we have enacted numerous laws to address the challenges facing American Indians and Alaska Natives. Most notable among these is the March 2013 reauthorization of the Violence Against Women Act, which strengthens provisions to address violence against American Indian and Alaska Native women. This reauthorization includes a critical new provision recognizing tribes' authority to prosecute in tribal courts those who commit acts of domestic violence on tribal lands irrespective of whether the perpetrator is Indian or non-Indian. Empowering indigenous peoples to address their challenges is a central principle of the UNDRIP, as well as sound policy. Additionally, a 2012 law gave greater control to tribes over tribal assets, including certain land leases, and a 2010 law enhances tribes' sentencing authority,

strengthens defendants' rights, establishes new guidelines and training for officers handling domestic violence and sex crimes, improves services to victims, and seeks to help combat alcohol and substance abuse and help at-risk youth.

60.　　We have prioritized reaching settlement agreements with Indian tribes over trust-mismanagement and other claims. These settlements to date total over $2.6 billion in compensation to more than 80 federally-recognized Indian tribes. In addition, we settled an individual trust case for $3.4 billion and settled a landmark class-action lawsuit by Indian farmers and ranchers alleging that they were discriminated against in federal agricultural programs.

E. Immigration

Detention of migrants and immigration policies
Recommendations 80, 82, 102, 144, 164, 183-185, and 212

61.　　On November 20, 2014, President Obama announced a series of executive actions on immigration and border security. These include: a plan to fundamentally alter our border security strategy; significant revisions to our immigration enforcement priorities; expansion of a policy to consider deferring removal, and providing work authorization, for certain individuals who arrived in the U.S. as children; and a new initiative to consider deferring removal, and providing work authorization, for certain parents of U.S. citizens and lawful permanent residents. Consistent with these actions, we are implementing a new enforcement and removal policy that continues to place top priority on threats to national security, public safety, and border security.

62.　　The United States continues to be a leader in extending protection to refugees and asylum seekers. In FY2014,[1] we admitted 69,987 refugees and granted asylum to 25,199 individuals. We have also substantially increased grants of immigration protection for victims of torture, trafficking, domestic violence, child abuse, abandonment, or neglect, and other qualifying crimes.

63.　　From 2010 to 2014, among individuals who either arrived or were apprehended near the border shortly after entering the country without permission, the number of people who expressed a fear of returning to their country of origin increased by 469 percent. Other screenings for fear of return have also markedly increased. To address the substantial increase in individuals seeking protection, we have hired nearly 150 new asylum officers since October 2013 and plan to hire more officers.

64.　　We are also taking action to address specific concerns regarding racial profiling and use of force at the U.S.-Mexico border. In May 2014, U.S. Customs and Border Protection publicly released an updated Use of Force Policy, Guidelines, and Procedures Handbook, which requires training in the use of safe tactics, a requirement to carry less-lethal devices, and guidance on responding to thrown projectiles. CBP is launching a use-of-force incident-tracking system to better inform its responses to incidents.

---

[1] Fiscal years begin on October 1 of the prior calendar year and end on September 30.

65.   The United States continues to provide due process guarantees throughout the immigration system, including in removal proceedings, where individuals are advised of their rights and other important information. While some individuals facing immigration proceedings are detained, that is only after an individualized determination that detention is appropriate or required by law. Many alternatives to detention are available and are used when appropriate. In FY2013, 37 percent of cases completed by the immigration courts involved an individual who was detained.

66.   Since our first UPR, we have promulgated the 2011 Performance-Based National Detention Standards, which cover many facilities housing immigration detainees and establish minimum conditions of detention, including with respect to medical care, access to legal resources, visitation, recreation, correspondence, religious services, and grievance processes.

67.   We have further prioritized the interview of and completion of asylum applications by unaccompanied children, consistent with the prioritization of the same population in immigration courts. Programs are being initiated to provide child advocates and representation to unaccompanied children in immigration proceedings in certain locations. We provide unaccompanied children with safe and appropriate residential environments until they are released to appropriate sponsors while their immigration cases proceed. While they are in our care, our facilities provide services such as food, clothes, basic education, recreation, and medical and legal assistance. Approximately 90 percent of all unaccompanied children were released to the care of a sponsor in FY2014. Once that occurs, they have a right under federal law – just like other children in their communities – to enroll in local public elementary and secondary schools, regardless of their or their sponsors' immigration status. We have also launched a program to provide refugee admission to certain children in El Salvador, Honduras, and Guatemala, providing a safe, orderly alternative to dangerous journeys from Central America.

Discrimination or violence against migrants and access to services
Recommendations 79, 104-105, 108, 165, 167, 207, 210, 214, and 220

68.   The United States has an unwavering commitment to respect the human rights of all migrants, regardless of their immigration status, and vigorously prosecutes crimes committed against migrants and enforces labor, workplace safety, and civil rights laws. All children have the right to equal access to public elementary and secondary education, regardless of their or their parents' immigration status, and such schools must provide meaningful access to their programs to persons with limited English proficiency, including migrants. In January 2015, we issued guidance to help schools ensure that English learner students can participate meaningfully and equally in education programs and services. Employers may not discriminate against employees or applicants based on their race, color, national origin, or, in certain cases, citizenship status.

69.   Regardless of immigration status, victims of domestic violence have full access to a network of 1,600 domestic violence shelters and other supportive services, including community health centers and substance abuse, mental health, and maternal and child health programs.

70.   VAWA specifically provides immigration protections for battered immigrants, allowing certain family members of U.S. citizens and lawful permanent residents who have been victims of domestic violence to independently petition for immigration status without the abuser's knowledge. This self-petitioning process removes one barrier to leaving that victims might face and shifts control over the immigration process to the victim, providing him or her with more options. In FY2014, 613 such self-petitions were granted.

71.   The DHS Traveler Redress Inquiry Program provides a way for travelers who experience difficulties during their travel screening to seek redress, including those who believe they have been unfairly or incorrectly delayed, denied boarding, or identified for additional screening as a result of being placed on the terrorist watchlist or its subset, the No Fly List. DHS TRIP works with other government agencies as appropriate to make an accurate determination about any traveler who has sought redress. We are actively reviewing and revising the existing redress program to increase transparency for certain individuals, consistent with the protection of national and transportation security and classified and other sensitive information.

Consular access and notification
Recommendations 54, 213, and 223

72.   The United States has made significant efforts to meet the goal of across-the-board compliance with its consular notification and access obligations under the Vienna Convention on Consular Relations. The Federal Rules of Criminal Procedure were amended in December 2014 to facilitate compliance with our consular notification and access obligations, requiring judges to notify all defendants at their initial appearance in a federal case that non-U.S. citizens may request that a consular officer from the defendant's country of nationality be notified of the arrest, but that even without a defendant's request, a treaty or other international agreement may require consular notification. We have distributed more than 200,000 manuals on consular notification and access, which provide detailed instructions for police and prison officials engaged in detention or arrest of a foreign national, in order to comply with the VCCR and all relevant bilateral consular agreements. We distribute other free consular notification and access training materials and post them online, and have conducted nearly 900 outreach and training sessions on consular notification and access since 1998.

73.   Legislation supported by the Administration that would bring us into compliance with the ICJ's judgment in *Avena* has previously been introduced in the Senate, but has not been enacted into law.

F. Labor and Trafficking

Gender equality in the workplace
Recommendation 115

74.　　U.S. law prohibits compensating men and women differently for the same or similar work, as well as any discrimination in compensation based on sex. However, the "gender gap" in pay persists. Full-time working women earn only about 78 percent of their male counterparts' earnings. We have established a high level task force to better respond to the issue, and continue to diligently enforce laws that address gender discrimination in pay in the workplace and seek justice for victims of sex-based wage discrimination.

75.　　For instance, from January 2010 to March 2013, the EEOC obtained more than $78 million in relief for such victims. From January 2010 to September 2014, DOL recovered more than $51 million in back wages and nearly 9,000 job opportunities on behalf of approximately 90,000 victims of discrimination, including gender discrimination. Additionally, in April 2014, President Obama signed an order prohibiting federal contractors from discriminating against employees who choose to discuss their compensation, and a Presidential Memorandum to advance equal pay through collection of compensation data collection. Private rights of action are also available to individuals who face gender discrimination in the workplace and wish to seek a remedy.

Human trafficking, including child prostitution
Recommendations 168-169

76.　　We remain committed to combatting human trafficking, including commercial sexual exploitation of children, and have made great progress since our last report. For example, in FY2013, DHS initiated 987 criminal investigations with a nexus to human trafficking, and obtained 1,028 indictments and 828 convictions on charges arising from trafficking investigations. In FY2014, we granted special permission to remain in the country to 18,520 victims of various crimes, including human trafficking, and their family members. We also continue to prepare educational materials about trafficking; in January 2015, we published a guide for educators and school staff about the indicators of possible human trafficking and how to address and prevent child exploitation.

77.　　We have streamlined federal human trafficking investigations and prosecutions and have collaborated on a bilateral initiative with Mexican law enforcement to dismantle sex trafficking networks. We also aggressively investigate and prosecute those who commit forced labor and sex trafficking. In FY2013, DOJ charged 163 defendants with forced labor or sex trafficking. In the three prior years, DOJ brought 221 such cases, compared to 149 in the previous four-year period and 82 in the four-year period before that.

78.　　In addition to criminal prosecutions, we continue to enforce the rights of trafficking victims. For example, in a set of cases related to a single employment broker, we obtained significant relief (including $3.6 million and injunctive relief) on behalf of approximately 500

Thai agricultural workers who were trafficked to the United States. In the settlement, one employer offered some of the workers full-time employment, including profit-sharing and retirement benefits.

79.   To assist trafficking victims in the United States, we have developed the first-ever Government-wide strategic action plan to strengthen services for trafficking victims, which is comprehensive, action-oriented, and designed to address the needs of all victims. Additionally, DHS has 26 full-time Victim Assistance Specialists in local investigative offices and more than 250 Victim Witness Coordinators. They work to ensure that possible human trafficking victims are rescued, transferred to safe locations, and provided with referrals for medical, mental health, and legal assistance.

Rights of agricultural and other workers
Recommendations 81, 192, and 193

80.   The United States vigorously enforces labor and employment laws without regard to a worker's immigration status. Furthermore, we combat employer efforts to discover the immigration status of workers during litigation, to prevent employers from threatening deportation, or otherwise intimidating workers or witnesses.

81.   We vigorously enforce laws that prohibit employment discrimination against migrant workers on the basis of race, color, national origin, sex, religion, age, disability, or genetic information. We have initiated and favorably resolved numerous cases on behalf of female farmworkers who were subjected to sexual harassment. Wage laws generally set basic minimum wage and overtime pay standards. Safety laws require safeguards to prevent worker injury. Environmental laws prescribe how certain chemicals must be handled in the workplace. Our laws also generally prohibit discrimination against covered persons based upon citizenship or immigration status in hiring, firing, recruitment, or referral for a fee.

82.   We have increased outreach to foreign workers, including agricultural workers, regarding their rights and how to pursue them, often by working cooperatively with NGOs and foreign governments—for example, through Consular Partnership agreements with a number of countries to provide information on U.S. labor and employment laws.

G. National Security

Counterterrorism efforts and intelligence-gathering
Recommendations 58, 59, 90, 187, 188, and 217

83.   The United States strives to protect privacy and civil liberties while also protecting national security. We have an extensive and effective framework of protections that applies to privacy and intelligence issues, including electronic surveillance. The Foreign Intelligence Surveillance Act governs, among other matters, electronic surveillance conducted within the United States for the purpose of gathering foreign intelligence or counterintelligence

information. In establishing the Foreign Intelligence Surveillance Court, FISA sets forth a system of rigorous, independent judicial oversight of the activities it regulates to ensure that they are lawful and effectively address privacy and civil liberties concerns. Such activities are also subject to oversight by the U.S. Congress and entities in our Executive Branch.

84.   Signals intelligence collection outside the FISA context is also regulated, and must have a valid foreign intelligence or counterintelligence purpose. In January 2014, the President issued Presidential Policy Directive-28, which enunciates standards for the collection and use of foreign signals intelligence. It emphasizes that we do not collect foreign intelligence for the purpose of suppressing criticism or dissent, or for disadvantaging any individual on the basis of ethnicity, race, gender, sexual orientation, or religion, and that agencies within our intelligence community are required to adopt and make public to the greatest extent feasible procedures for the protection of personal information of non-U.S. persons. It also requires that privacy and civil liberties protections be integral in the planning of those activities, and that personal information be protected at appropriate stages of collection, retention, and dissemination.

85.   PPD-28 recognizes that all persons should be treated with dignity and respect, regardless of nationality or place of residence, and that all persons have legitimate privacy interests in the handling of their personal information collected through signals intelligence. It therefore requires U.S. signals intelligence activities to include appropriate safeguards for the personal information of all individuals.

86.   Further, our intelligence community is required to report on such programs and activities to Congress, where these issues are vigorously debated. Agencies within our intelligence community have privacy and civil liberties officers. The National Security Agency, for example, has recently established a Civil Liberties and Privacy Officer who advises on issues including signals intelligence programs that entail the collection of personal information.

Military detention and transfer, operations, and accountability
Recommendations 60, 66, 88, 89, 136-140, 142, 143, 146-149, 155-161, 166, 176, and 218

87.   The United States is fully committed to ensuring that individuals it detains in any armed conflict are treated humanely. All U.S. military detention operations conducted in connection with armed conflict, including at Guantanamo Bay, are carried out in accordance with U.S. law, international humanitarian law including Common Article 3 of the Geneva Conventions of 1949, and other international laws, including the Convention Against Torture, as applicable.

88.   The President has repeatedly reaffirmed his commitment to close the Guantanamo Bay detention facility. There were 242 detainees at Guantanamo at the beginning of this Administration. Since then, 116 have been transferred out of the facility, including 28 in 2014 and an additional five in January 2015. Currently, 122 detainees remain at Guantanamo, 54 of whom are designated for transfer. Out of the 68 others, ten are currently facing charges or serving criminal sentences; and the remaining 58 are eligible for review by the Periodic Review Board, which commenced in October 2013. The PRB has already conducted 12 hearings and two six-month file reviews, in which detainees participated with assistance from their personal

representatives and private counsel. The PRB determined that continued detention of six of these detainees is no longer necessary, making them eligible for transfer, subject to appropriate security measures and consistent with our humane transfer policy. Two of these detainees have already been transferred to their countries of origin.

89.   Under our standard military procedures, individuals detained by U.S. forces for more than 14 days are assigned an Internment Serial Number, starting a formal process of oversight and record keeping. Every ISN is reported to the International Committee of the Red Cross, and the ICRC is given access to these individuals as well as to all internment locations, including Guantanamo Bay, which the ICRC has visited more than 100 times since 2002.

90.   All Guantanamo detainees can file a petition in U.S. federal court challenging the lawfulness of their detention. They have access to counsel and appropriate information to mount such a challenge.

91.   Torture and cruel, inhuman or degrading treatment or punishment by U.S. personnel is prohibited at all times and in all places without exception. Immediately upon taking office in 2009, President Obama issued an Executive Order on ensuring lawful interrogations, which mandated that, consistent with the CAT and Common Article 3 of the 1949 Geneva Conventions, any individual detained in armed conflict by the United States or within a facility owned, operated, or controlled by the United States, in all circumstances, must be treated humanely. This Executive Order revoked legal opinions, including regarding the definition of torture, that previously had been relied upon in the context of the former CIA detention and interrogation program, which was ended by President Obama.

92.   As a matter of fundamental policy and practice, we do not transfer any individual to a foreign country if it is more likely than not that the person would be tortured, after considering the totality of relevant factors. These include any allegations of prior or potential mistreatment of the individual by the receiving government, the receiving country's human rights record, whether post-transfer detention is contemplated, the specific factors suggesting that the individual in question is at risk of being tortured by officials in that country, whether similarly situated individuals have been tortured by the country under consideration, and, where applicable, any diplomatic assurances of humane treatment from the receiving country, including an assessment of their credibility. With respect to law of war detainee transfers, and in other contexts in which assurances are sought, it is U.S. practice to seek consistent, private access for post-transfer monitoring where post-transfer detention by the receiving state is anticipated, with minimal advance notice to the detaining government.

93.   U.S. government personnel who are responsible for conducting interrogations receive training and are prohibited under U.S. law and policy from engaging in torture or cruel, inhuman, or degrading treatment, regardless of location. The Detainee Treatment Act of 2005, for example, prohibits subjecting persons detained under the law of war by the Department of Defense, or in a DoD facility, to any interrogation technique that is not authorized by and listed in U.S. Army Field Manual 2.22-3, and this prohibition is extended by executive order to all U.S. agencies detaining individuals in any armed conflict. Interrogations that comply with that Manual are consistent with U.S. and international legal obligations.

94.   DoD has multiple accountability mechanisms in place to ensure that personnel adhere to law and policy in military operations and detention. DoD has conducted thousands of investigations and prosecuted or disciplined hundreds of service members for mistreatment of detainees and other related misconduct since 2001.

95.   Regarding civilian prosecutions for potential abuses committed in armed conflict since September 11, 2001, DOJ conducted an extensive review led by Assistant U.S. Attorney John Durham of the treatment of 101 persons alleged to have been mistreated while in U.S. custody since the 9/11 attacks. That review generated two criminal investigations, but after examining a broad universe of allegations from multiple sources, the prosecutor concluded that the admissible evidence would not have been sufficient to obtain and sustain convictions beyond a reasonable doubt. DOJ has brought two cases and obtained convictions against two contractors for abuse of detainees in Afghanistan.

96.   In December 2014, the U.S. Senate Select Committee on Intelligence released a declassified Executive Summary of its Report on the CIA's former detention and interrogation program. Harsh interrogation techniques highlighted in that Report are not representative of how the United States deals with the threat of terrorism today, and are not consistent with our values. The United States supports transparency and has taken steps to ensure that it never resorts to the use of those techniques again.

97.   We are currently making efforts to accommodate Special Rapporteur on Torture Juan Mendez's request for a country visit. Last fall, we confirmed with Mr. Mendez our willingness to facilitate a visit to state and local facilities, per his request. With regard to his request to visit the Guantanamo Bay detention facility, we have extended an invitation for him to tour the facility and to observe operations there under the same conditions as other visitors, aside from the ICRC, which has regular access to Guantanamo detainees as described in Paragraph 89.

98.   The United States continues to employ military commissions for the prosecution of certain offenses committed in the context of, and in association with, hostilities. All current military commission proceedings are required under U.S. law to apply fair trial safeguards, including the presumption of innocence; prohibitions on the use of evidence obtained by cruel, inhuman, or degrading treatment; restrictions on the admissibility of hearsay evidence and statements of the accused; the accused's right to discovery of evidence; and the standard of proving guilt beyond a reasonable doubt. A conviction by a military commission is subject to multiple layers of review, including judicial review by civilian courts. In order to increase transparency and accountability, proceedings are now transmitted via video feed to locations at Guantanamo Bay and in the United States, so that the press and the public can view them with a 40-second delay to protect against the disclosure of classified information.

99.   Finally, the United States takes scrupulous care to ensure that the use of military force, including through use of unmanned aerial vehicles, complies with the law of war, including the principles of distinction and proportionality. In addition, before we take any counterterrorism strike outside areas of active hostilities, it is U.S. policy that there must be near-certainty that no civilians will be killed or injured. Our counterterrorism policy requires that if at any time during

the targeting process outside areas of active hostilities capture appears feasible, we must pursue capture instead; our preference is to detain, interrogate, and to prosecute when feasible.

H. Economic, Social, and Cultural Measures

Access to food and healthcare
Recommendations 195-196

100.   The United States has undertaken many initiatives domestically to promote food security and expand health care. The Affordable Care Act has increased health coverage options and quality through new consumer protections, the creation of the Health Insurance Marketplaces—a new means for uninsured people to enroll in health coverage—and additional support for state Medicaid and Children's Health Insurance Programs. It requires most health plans to cover ten categories of essential health benefits, including preventive services, maternity and prenatal care, hospitalizations, and mental health and substance use disorder services. It also reauthorized the Indian Healthcare Improvement Act, to address some of the health care access concerns in indigenous communities.

101.   We are committed to expanding access to health care to all our citizens and as such, have made efforts to strengthen and protect our social and health care programs: Medicare for the elderly and disabled, and Medicaid for low-income individuals and families. Under the ACA, Medicare beneficiaries have saved billions of dollars on prescription drugs and have seen no increase in rates since 2013. Additionally, Medicare beneficiaries no longer have to pay cost-sharing for preventive services, and nearly nine million individuals have enrolled in coverage in state-run Medicaid programs since October 2013.

102.   In FY2014, we invested more than $103 billion in domestic food assistance programs, serving one in four Americans during the year. Beneficiaries included about 46.5 million low-income individuals each month under the Supplemental Nutrition Assistance Program; about 8.3 million per month under the Special Supplemental Nutrition Program for Women, Infants and Children; over 30.3 million children each school day; and over 2.5 million elderly adults each year through the Older Americans Act nutrition programs. Emergency food providers received 785 million pounds of food through the Emergency Food Assistance Program. Substantial evidence demonstrates that these programs improve social, economic, and nutrition conditions for low-income Americans.

Access to education
Recommendation 109

103.   We are committed to equality of opportunity in education and to helping students succeed in school, careers, and life. To help increase educational excellence, support innovation and improvement, and address continuing challenges, ED has dedicated well over $1 billion to early childhood education, and also has launched a number of other programs and initiatives, including the Excellent Educators for All Initiative in July 2014, which directs states to submit plans in

2015 to help ensure that poor and minority children have equal access to experienced, qualified teachers. Also in 2014, we issued guidance to states, school districts, and schools to help ensure that students have equal access to educational resources, and launched the Performance Partnership Pilots program to test innovative, outcome-focused strategies for achieving significant improvements in educational, employment, and other key outcomes for disconnected youth.

104.   In 2013, we issued guidance to institutions of higher education to help them promote diversity on their campuses. Guidance was also issued for elementary and secondary schools, school districts, and higher education institutions seeking to achieve a diverse student body. See Paragraphs 30-32 on racial discrimination in education.

Homelessness and access to housing, water, and sanitation
Recommendations 113 and 197

105.   *Housing and homelessness*—The United States is committed to ending homelessness, and has made great progress in this area. For example, in 2010, we launched Opening Doors, a strategic plan aimed at ending homelessness among veterans by the end of 2015; chronic homelessness by 2016; and homelessness for families, youth, and children by 2020; and setting a path to eradicate all types of homelessness in the United States. HUD's statistics show that since that launch, chronic homelessness has dropped 21 percent, homelessness among families has declined 15 percent, and homelessness among veterans has fallen by 33 percent. In 2016, the new National Housing Trust Fund is expected to begin distributing funds to increase and preserve affordable housing for very low-income and homeless individuals. Additionally, federal law guarantees immediate access to a free appropriate public education for children and youth experiencing homelessness.

106.   *Water and sanitation*—In 2013, we competitively awarded $12.7 million to public water systems and wastewater systems. The funding helps provide water system staff with training and tools to enhance system operations and management practices, and it supports our continuing efforts to protect public health and promote sustainability in small communities. Through the U.S.-Mexico Border Water Infrastructure Grant Program, the United States and Mexico have been addressing critical water and sanitation infrastructure problems in the border region. During 2010-14, the program provided drinking water connections to 34,307 homes and wastewater connections to 403,634 homes. Between 2009 and 2013, we provided an additional 12,676 homes of indigenous persons with access to safe drinking water to decrease the risk of illness and improve quality of life.

Foreign and humanitarian assistance
Recommendations 52, 226, and 227

107.   Between October 2010 and September 2014, the United States provided more than $800 million in foreign assistance in response to natural disasters, nearly $400 million in disaster preparedness and risk reduction activities, and over $22 billion in humanitarian assistance out of

a foreign assistance budget of over $207 billion during that period. Despite recent reductions in the foreign assistance budget, our response to natural disasters has remained steadfast, and we continue to be an international leader in both disaster response and preparedness.

108.   As underscored by the "Leahy law," our partner nations' security forces' respect for human rights is critical. In 2014, the DoD "Leahy law" expanded the prohibition on DoD-funded activities to include not only training but also equipment and "other assistance" for members of a unit of a foreign security force for which there is credible information that the unit has committed a gross violation of human rights.

I. Environment
Recommendations 51, 221, and 222

109.   The United States is firmly committed to addressing the causes and impacts of climate change. The National Environmental Policy Act requires federal agencies to incorporate environmental considerations in their planning and decision-making processes. The President's Climate Action Plan has committed to cut carbon pollution and other greenhouse emissions; promote renewable energy development and use; cut waste in homes, businesses, and factories; conserve land and water resources; use sound science to manage climate impacts; launch a climate resilience toolkit and climate data initiative; and actively engage in international efforts to address global climate change.

110.   Our new fuel economy standards for certain vehicles will reduce carbon pollution by over six billion tons, and we support renewable fuel standards and research and development investments to bring next-generation bio-fuels to the energy market. We are also working to reduce our greenhouse gas emissions from direct sources, such as facility energy use and fuel consumption by 28 percent by 2020, and to reduce our greenhouse gas emissions from indirect sources, such as employee commuting, by 13 percent by 2020.

111.   As part of our domestic efforts to address climate change, we continue to focus attention on the environmental and health conditions of minority, low-income, and indigenous communities. This includes understanding the implications of climate change impacts on members of domestic minority, low-income, and indigenous communities; identifying populations and communities vulnerable to climate change; and seeking meaningful involvement and fair treatment of all our people, regardless of race, color, national origin, or income, in the design and evaluation of adaptation strategies.

112.   Internationally, we are helping vulnerable countries adapt to climate change and enhance resilience of their communities and economies, including by providing $2.2 billion in adaptation assistance from 2010-2014. We are currently working toward an ambitious, effective, and inclusive global climate change agreement in 2015 under which all countries would make emission reduction contributions.

J. Treaties and International Human Rights Mechanisms

Ratification of and reservations to human rights instruments
Recommendations 1-11, 13-30, 33-35, 37-45, and 47-49

113.   The United States is a party to numerous human rights treaties, and our reservations, understandings, and declarations to these treaties are limited, necessary, compatible with the objects and purposes of the respective instruments, and do not undermine compliance with our obligations.

114.   Although we have not ratified any new human rights treaties since our last Report, we have taken steps to ratify the Convention on the Rights of Persons with Disabilities. The United States signed the CRPD in 2009 and transmitted it to the Senate for advice and consent to ratification in 2012. The Administration continues to support ratification of the CRPD with the reservations, understandings, and declarations included in the resolution of advice and consent passed by the Senate Foreign Relations Committee.

115.   We support ratification of the Convention on the Elimination of All Forms of Discrimination Against Women, and have designated CEDAW as a priority among multilateral treaties for ratification. The United States signed CEDAW in 1979, and the President transmitted it to the Senate for advice and consent to ratification in 1980. The principles endorsed in CEDAW are consistent with our domestic and foreign policy objectives and are strongly supported in federal and state law.

116.   The United States steadfastly supports the International Labour Organization Declaration on Fundamental Principles and Rights at Work. In the context of the Follow-up to the Declaration, we have demonstrated that U.S. workers enjoy those fundamental principles and rights. In May 2014, the President's Committee on the ILO pledged to redouble its efforts to ratify Convention 111 on Discrimination in Employment and Occupation, demonstrating our commitment to equal opportunity and treatment and the elimination of employment discrimination worldwide.

117.   The United States is one of the strongest supporters of the Inter-American human rights system, and is the largest donor country to the Inter-American Commission on Human Rights. We actively participate in IACHR hearings and afford due consideration to the IACHR's recommendations.

Special procedures
Recommendation 93

118.   The United States accepts country visit requests by Special Procedures mandate holders as scheduling allows and has hosted nine such visits in the past five years. Also see Paragraph 97.

IV.   Conclusion

119.   The United States has a long history of promoting, protecting, and respecting human rights, beginning with our Declaration of Independence and our Constitution. We remain committed to improving implementation of our human rights obligations and commitments, through laws, policies, programs, training, and other mechanisms.

120.   The United States is committed to an open, inclusive, and transparent review before the UPR working group, and continues to support strongly the UPR process and the UN human rights system. We look forward to hearing the recommendations of states, with a view to continuing our improvement and strengthening of human rights protections, in cooperation with civil society and the international community.

Annex I: Abbreviations

ACA	Affordable Care Act
CAT	Convention Against Torture and Other Cruel, Inhuman or Degrading Treatment or Punishment
CEDAW	Convention on the Elimination of All Forms of Discrimination Against Women
CIA	U.S. Central Intelligence Agency
CRPD	Convention on the Rights of Persons with Disabilities
DHS	U.S. Department of Homeland Security
DHS TRIP	U.S. Department of Homeland Security Traveler Redress Inquiry Program
DoD	U.S. Department of Defense
DOI	U.S. Department of the Interior
DOJ	U.S. Department of Justice
DOL	U.S. Department of Labor
ED	U.S. Department of Education
EEOC	U.S. Equal Employment Opportunity Commission
FISA	Foreign Intelligence Surveillance Act
HHS	U.S. Department of Health and Human Services
HUD	U.S. Department of Housing and Urban Development
IACHR	Inter-American Commission on Human Rights
ICRC	International Committee of the Red Cross
ILO	International Labour Organization
ISN	Internment Serial Number
LGBT	Lesbian, gay, bisexual and transgender
NGO	Non-governmental organization
NHRI	National Human Rights Institution
PPD-28	Presidential Policy Directive 28 – Signals Intelligence Activities
PRB	Periodic Review Board
UNDRIP	UN Declaration on the Rights of Indigenous Peoples
UPR	Universal Periodic Review
USSC	U.S. Sentencing Commission
VAWA	Violence Against Women Act
VCCR	Vienna Convention on Consular Relations

Annex II: Selected Civil Society Consultations

Topic	Date	Location
Convention on the Rights of the Child Protocols	Oct. 31, 2012	Washington, DC
Convention on the Rights of the Child Protocols	Jan. 15, 2013	Geneva, Switzerland
International Covenant on Civil and Political Rights (ICCPR)	Jan 10, 2012	Washington, DC
International Covenant on Civil and Political Rights (ICCPR)	May 30, 2013	Washington, DC
International Covenant on Civil and Political Rights (ICCPR)	March 12, 2014	Geneva, Switzerland
Access to Justice	April 1, 2014	Washington, DC
Indigenous Issues	April 24, 2014	Norman, Oklahoma
Civil Rights, Non-Discrimination, and Criminal Justice	July 9, 2012	Washington, DC
Civil Rights and Non-Discrimination	July 8, 2014	Washington, DC
Criminal Justice Issues	July 9, 2014	Washington, DC
Human Rights Treaties	Aug. 1, 2014	Washington, DC
Convention on the Elimination of Racial Discrimination (CERD)	Aug. 12, 2014	Geneva, Switzerland
Immigration, Trafficking, and Labor	Sept. 12, 2014	Washington, DC
Environmental Issues	Oct. 7, 2014	Berkeley, California
National Security	Oct. 14, 2014	Washington, DC
Convention Against Torture (CAT)	Oct. 14, 2014	Washington, DC
Convention Against Torture (CAT)	Nov. 11, 2014	Geneva, Switzerland
National Congress of American Indians	June 18-19, 2012	Lincoln, Nebraska
National Association of Counties	July 13-17, 2012	Pittsburgh, PA

Annex III: Participating U.S. Federal Agencies

U.S. Department of Agriculture (USDA)

U.S. Department of Defense (DoD)

U.S. Department of Education (ED)

U.S. Department of Health and Human Services (HHS)

U.S. Department of Homeland Security (DHS)

U.S. Department of Housing and Urban Development (HUD)

U.S. Department of the Interior (DOI)

U.S. Department of Justice (DOJ)

U.S. Department of Labor (DOL)

U.S. Department of State (DOS)

U.S. Environmental Protection Agency (EPA)

U.S. Equal Employment Opportunity Commission (EEOC)

U.S. Interagency Council on Homelessness (USICH)

U.S. National Labor Relations Board (NLRB)

U.S. Office of the Director of National Intelligence (ODNI)

Annex IV: First Cycle UPR Recommendations Supported in Whole or in Part by the United States

Note: This document compiles in one place both the text of the recommendations supported by the United States during the first Universal Periodic Review (UPR) cycle, as they were listed in the UPR Working Group's January 2011 Report (A/HRC/16/11), and the comments and positions the United States articulated on those recommendations in its March 2011 response (A/HRC/16/11/Add.1). Because the second UPR cycle will focus on recommendations supported by the United States, this document omits those recommendations that the United States did *not* support in 2011. Although the titles of some headings and placement of some of the recommendations have been altered slightly, the recommendations, responses, and general substance remain unchanged.

GENERAL COMMENTS

Some recommendations ask the United States to achieve an ideal, e.g., end discrimination or police brutality, and others request action not entirely under the control of our Federal Executive Branch, e.g., adopt legislation, ratify particular treaties, or take action at the state level. Such recommendations enjoy our support, or our support in part, when we share the ideal that the recommendations express, are making serious efforts toward achieving their goals, and intend to continue to do so. Nonetheless, we recognize, realistically, that the United States may never completely accomplish what is described in the literal terms of the recommendation. We are also comfortable supporting a recommendation to do something that we already do, and intend to continue doing, without in any way implying that we agree with a recommendation that understates the success of our ongoing efforts.

Some countries added to their recommendations inaccurate assumptions, assertions, or factual predicates, some of which are contrary to the spirit of the UPR. In such cases, we have decided whether we support a recommendation by looking past the rhetoric to the specific action or objective being proposed. When we say we "support in part" such recommendations, we mean that we support the proposed action or objective but reject the often provocative assumption or assertion embedded in the recommendation.

The recommendations have been divided into ten subject matter categories:

(1) Civil Rights, Ethnic, and Racial Discrimination
(2) Criminal Justice Issues
(3) Indigenous Issues
(4) National Security
(5) Immigration
(6) Labor and Trafficking
(7) Economic, Social and Cultural Rights and Measures
(8) The Environment
(9) Domestic Implementation of Human Rights
(10) Treaties and International Human Rights Mechanisms

1. CIVIL RIGHTS, ETHNIC, AND RACIAL DISCRIMINATION

Recommendations the United States Supports:

Recommendations 68, 101, and 219: (68) Take legislative and administrative measures to ban racial profiling in law enforcement; (101) Ban, at the federal and state levels, the use of racial profiling by police and immigration officers; Prohibit expressly the use of racial profiling in the enforcement of immigration legislation; (219) Enact a national legislation that prohibits religious, racial and color profiling particularly in context of the fight against terrorism.

> **U.S. position**: Profiling – the invidious use of race, ethnicity, national origin, or religion – is prohibited under the U.S. Constitution and numerous pieces of national legislation.

Recommendation 95: Undertake studies to determine the factors of racial disparity in the application of the death penalty, to prepare effective strategies aimed at ending possible discriminatory practices.

Recommendation 96: Take appropriate legislative and practical measures to prevent racial bias in the criminal justice system.

Recommendation 97: Review the minimum mandatory sentences in order to assess their disproportionate impact on the racial and ethnic minorities.

Recommendation 106: Take administrative and legal measures against perpetrators of racially motivated acts, targeting migrants and minority communities.

> **U.S. position**: We support this recommendation insofar as it involves enforcing our laws, e.g., hate crimes legislation, and taking appropriate administrative actions.

Recommendations 107 and 111: (107) Adopt effective measures and an anti-discrimination act to address racial problems; (111) Adopt a comprehensive national work-plan to combat racial discrimination.

> **U.S. position**: We have comprehensive Federal and State legislation and strategies to combat racial discrimination. We are working diligently toward better enforcement and implementation of these laws and programs.

Recommendations 86 and 112: (86) Undertake awareness-raising campaigns for combating stereotypes and violence against gays, lesbians, bisexuals and transsexuals, and ensure access to public services paying attention to the special vulnerability of sexual workers to violence and human rights abuses; (112) Take measures to comprehensively address discrimination against individuals on the basis of their sexual orientation or gender identity.

> **U.S. position**: We agree that no one should face violence or discrimination in access to public services based on sexual orientation or their status as a person in prostitution, as these recommendations suggest. We have recently taken concrete steps to address discrimination on the basis of sexual orientation and gender identity, and are engaged in further efforts.

Recommendation 114: Increase its efforts to effectively guarantee human rights of persons with disabilities, while welcoming the signing of the Convention and urging their prompt implementation.

Recommendation 116: Continue its intense efforts to undertake all necessary measures to ensure fair and equal treatment of all persons, without regard to sex, race, religion, colour, creed, sexual orientation, gender identity or disability, and encourage further steps in this regard.

Recommendation 144: Increases its efforts to eliminate alleged brutality and use of excessive force by law enforcement officials against, inter alia, Latino and African American persons and undocumented migrants, and to ensure that relevant allegations are investigated and that perpetrators are prosecuted.

U.S. position: We support this recommendation insofar as it allows for the exercise of prosecutorial discretion.

Recommendation 151: Strengthen oversight with a view to ending excessive use of force by law enforcement bodies, particularly when it is directed to the racial minorities and bring those responsible for violation of laws to justice.

Recommendation 167: Take effective steps to put an end to child prostitution, and effectively combat violence against women and gun violence.

Recommendation 191: Continue to create an enabling climate for religious and cultural tolerance and understanding at the grass roots level.

Recommendation 198: Reinforce the broad range of safeguards in favor of the most vulnerable groups such as persons with disabilities and the homeless to allow them the full enjoyment of their rights and dignity.

Recommendation 209: Guarantee the prohibition of use of cruelty and excessive or fatal force by law enforcement officials against people of Latin American or African origin as well as illegal migrants and to investigate such cases of excessive use of force.

> **U.S. position**: Law enforcement and immigration officers are lawfully permitted to use deadly force under certain exceptional circumstances; e.g., self-defense or defense of another person.

Recommendations the United States Supports in Part:

Recommendation 62: Review, reform and adequate its federal and state laws, in consultation with civil society, to comply with the protection of the right to nondiscrimination established by the Convention on the Elimination of all Forms of Racial Discrimination (CERD), especially in the areas of employment, housing, health, education and justice.

> **U.S. position**: We disagree with some of the premises embedded in this recommendation, but we are committed to the objectives it states, in this case combating discrimination and promoting tolerance. While we recognize there is always room for improvement, we believe that our law is consistent with our CERD obligations. (See also the explanation of our positions regarding recommendations 65, 107, and 111.)

Recommendations 64, 67, 94, 98, 100, and 189: (64) Review, with a view to their amendment and elimination, all laws and practices that discriminate against African, Arab and Muslim Americans, as well as migrants, in the administration of justice, including racial and religious profiling; (67) Take legislative and administrative measures to address a wide range of racial discrimination and inequalities in housing, employment and education; (94) End the discrimination against persons of African descent; (98) Devise specific programs aimed at countering growing Islamophobic and xenophobic trends in society; (100) End all forms of racial discrimination in terms of housing, education, health care, social security and labor; (189) Consider discontinuing measures that curtail human rights and fundamental freedoms.

> **U.S. position**: See general comments, as well as the explanation of our positions regarding recommendations 107 and 111.

Recommendation 99: Eliminate discrimination against migrants and religious and ethnic minorities and ensure equal opportunity for enjoyment of their economic, social and cultural rights.

U.S. position: A migrant's eligibility for full benefits under certain programs may depend on his/her lawful status.

Recommendation 103: Ensure the prosecution and punishment, according to the law, of those responsible of racial hate and xenophobic criminal acts, as well as guarantee a fair compensation to the victims, such as the case of the Ecuadoreans Marcelo Lucero and Jose Sucuzhañay, murdered in the United States.

U.S. position: We support the recommendation as it regards investigating and, where appropriate, prosecuting persons who violate criminal laws. We cannot support the part of the recommendation asking that we "guarantee a fair compensation." Although mechanisms for remedies are available through our courts, we cannot make commitments regarding outcomes.

Recommendation 190: Take effective measures to counter insults against Islam and Holy Quran, as well as Islamophobia and violence against Moslems, and adopt necessary legislation.

U.S. position: We take effective measures to counter intolerance, violence, and discrimination against all members of all minority groups, including Muslims. We cannot support this recommendation, however, to the extent that it asks us to take legislative measures countering insults. Insults (unlike discrimination, threats, or violence) are speech protected by our Constitution.

2. CRIMINAL JUSTICE ISSUES

Recommendations the United States Supports:

Recommendation 70: Take appropriate legislative and practical measures to improve living conditions through its prisons systems, in particular with regard to access to health care and education.

Recommendation 145: Guarantee the complete prohibition of torture in all prisons under its control.

U.S. position: U.S. law prohibits torture in all prisons and detention facilities under its control.

Recommendation 152: Prevent and repress the illegitimate use of violence against detainees.

U.S. position: U.S. law prohibits mistreatment of detainees in U.S. custody, requires investigations of credible mistreatment allegations, and prescribes accountability measures for violations.

Recommendation 162: Redouble its efforts to address sexual violence in correction and detention facilities as well as to address the problem of prison conditions, with a view to preserving the rights and dignity of all those deprived of their liberty.

Recommendation 163: Reduce overcrowding in prisons by enlarging existing facilities or building new ones and/or making more use of alternative penalties.

Recommendation 177: Ensure the full enjoyment of human rights by persons deprived of their liberty, including by way of ensuring treatment in maximum security prisons in conformity with international law.

Recommendation 179: Review of alternative ways to handle petty crime and of measures to improve the situation of inmates in prisons.

Recommendations the United States Supports in Part:

Recommendation 118: A national moratorium on the death penalty is introduced with a view to completely abolish the penalty and, before such a moratorium is introduced, to take all necessary measures to ensure that any use of the death penalty complies with minimum standards under international law relating to the death penalty such as under article 6 and 14 of the International Covenant on Civil and Political Rights.

> **U.S. position**: We will continue to ensure that implementation of the death penalty complies with our international obligations; the portion asking that we end capital punishment does not enjoy our support.

Recommendations 134 and 135: (134) End the prosecution and execution of mentally-ill persons and minors; (135) Extend the exclusion of death penalty to all crimes committed by persons with mental illness.

> **U.S. position**: We cannot support Recommendation 134 with respect to prosecution. We support both recommendations with respect to executions regarding minors and persons with certain intellectual disabilities, but not regarding all persons with any mental illness.

Recommendation 150: Take measures with a view to prohibiting and punishing the brutality and the use of excessive or deadly force by the law enforcement officials and to banning torture and other ill-treatment in its detention facilities at home and abroad.

> **U.S. position**: See general comments, as well as explanations of the U.S. position for recommendations 145, 208, and 209.

Recommendation 173: Comply with the principles of international cooperation, as defined in Resolution 3074 of the General Assembly, for the extradition of persons accused of crimes against humanity and proceed to extradite former Bolivian authorities that are legally accused of such crimes, in order to be brought to trial in their country of origin.

> **U.S. position**: The first part of this recommendation enjoys our support; we cannot support the recommendation's second part ("proceed to extradite former Bolivian authorities…"). In addition, decisions on extradition cases are made on a case-by-case basis, consistent with our international legal obligations, and the United States cannot prejudge the outcome of any particular case.

Recommendations 174 and 175: (174) Make those responsible for gross violations of human rights in American prisons and prisons under the jurisdiction of America outside its territory accountable, compensate victims and provide them with remedies; (175) Put on trial its gross violators of human rights and its war criminals and accede to ICC.

> **U.S. position**: See general comments. In addition, we are committed to holding accountable persons responsible for human rights violations and war crimes. We cannot, however, support the portion of Recommendation 174 regarding compensation and remedies, because those are not always applicable. Nor can we support the part of Recommendation 175 that we accede to the Rome Statute, although we are engaging with State Parties to the Rome Statute on issues of concern.

Recommendation 178: Ensure the enjoyment of the right to vote both by persons deprived of their liberty and of persons who have completed their prison sentences.

> **U.S. position**: We support this recommendation to the extent that some State laws conform to it. Most inmates do not have the right to vote, however, and former felons do not have the right to vote in some States.

Recommendation 186: Ensure the right to habeas corpus in all cases of detention.
> **U.S. position**: We support this recommendation to the extent provided for under the U.S. Constitution and U.S. laws, and consistent with our international obligations.

3. INDIGENOUS ISSUES

Recommendations the United States Supports:

Recommendations 83, 200, 202, 203, 205, and 206: (83) Implement concrete measures consistent with the Covenant on Civil and Political Rights, to ensure the participation of indigenous peoples in the decisions affecting their natural environment, measures of subsistence, culture and spiritual practices; (200) Guarantee the rights of indigenous Americans, and to fully implement the United Nations Declaration on the Rights of Indigenous Peoples; (202) Adopt and implement the United Nations Declaration on the Rights of Indigenous Peoples; (203) Endorse the United Nations Declaration on the Rights of Indigenous Peoples when completing its national review process; (205) Continue its forward movement on the Declaration of the Rights of Indigenous Peoples; (206) Guarantee the full enjoyment of the rights on natives of America in line with the United Nations Declaration on the Rights of Indigenous Peoples.

> **U.S. position**: We support these recommendations consistent with the "Announcement of U.S. Support for the United Nations Declaration on the Rights of Indigenous Peoples – Initiatives to Promote the Government-to-Government Relationship & Improve the Lives of Indigenous Peoples."

Recommendation 85: Formulate goals and policy guidelines for the promotion of the rights of indigenous peoples and cooperation between government and indigenous peoples.

Recommendations the United States Supports in Part:

Recommendation 199: End the violation of the rights of indigenous peoples.

> **U.S. position**: See general comments.

Recommendation 201: Recognize the United Nations Declaration on the Rights of Indigenous Peoples without conditions or reservations, and implement it at the federal and state levels.

> **U.S. position**: We cannot accept the first part of this recommendation ("Recognize … without conditions"), but the second part ("implement …") enjoys our support, consistent with the "Announcement of U.S. Support for the United Nations Declaration on the Rights of Indigenous Peoples – Initiatives to Promote the Government-to-Government Relationship & Improve the Lives of Indigenous Peoples."

4. NATIONAL SECURITY

Recommendations the United States Supports:

Recommendations 58 and 176: (58) Make fully consistent all domestic anti-terrorism legislation and action with human rights standards; (176) Respect the human rights of prisoners of war, guaranteed by the penal norms.

> **U.S. position**: We support these recommendations insofar as they recommend compliance with our international law obligations.

Recommendations 66 and 146: (66): Enact a federal crime of torture, consistent with the Convention, and also encompassing acts described as 'enhanced interrogation techniques'; (146) Define torture as a federal offense in line with the Convention against Torture and investigate, prosecute and punish those responsible of crimes of extraterritorial torture.

> **U.S. position**: Existing Federal criminal laws comply with our obligations under the Convention against Torture.

Recommendation 89: Consider the possibility of inviting relevant mandate holders as follow up to the 2006 joint-study by the 5 special procedures, in view of the decision of the current Administration to close the Guantanamo Bay detention facility.

Recommendation 90: Respond and follow-up appropriately the recommendations formulated to the United States by the Special Rapporteur for the Protection of Human Rights and Fundamental Freedoms while Countering Terrorism.

Recommendation 139: That measures be taken to eradicate all forms of torture and ill treatment of detainees by military or civilian personnel, in any territory of jurisdiction, and that any such acts be thoroughly investigated.

Recommendation 149: Observe the Amnesty International 12 points program to prevent torture perpetrated by government agents.

> **U.S. position**: Some of the referenced points may not be fully applicable in every context.

Recommendations 159 and 160: (159) Close without any delay all detention facilities at the Guantanamo Bay as President Barack Obama has promised; (160) Find for all persons still detained in the Guantanamo Bay detention center a solution in line with the United States obligations regarding the foundations of international and human rights law, in particular with the International Covenant on Civil and Political Rights.

> **U.S. position**: We have made clear our desire to close the Guantánamo Bay detention facility and will continue to work with Congress, the courts, and other countries to do so in a responsible manner that is consistent with our international obligations. Until it is closed, this Administration will continue to ensure that operations there are consistent with our international legal obligations.

Recommendation 161: Halt all transfer detainees to third countries unless there are adequate safeguards to ensure that they will be treated in accordance with international law requirements.

Recommendation 188: Adopt a set of legislative and administrative measures aimed at ensuring prohibition of the use by state and local authorities of modern technology for excessive and unjustified intervention in citizens' private life.

> **U.S. position**: The U.S. Constitution's Fourth Amendment and existing U.S. law prohibit the use of modern technology for excessive and unjustified interference in individuals' private lives.

Recommendation 218: Do not prosecute those arrested for terrorist crimes or any other crime in exceptional tribunals or jurisdictions, but bring them to judicial instances legally established, with the protection of due process and under all the guarantees of the American Constitution.

> **U.S. position**: Persons who are charged with terrorist-related crimes are tried under legally established processes in either civilian courts or military commissions, depending on the nature of the crime and the individual. They are afforded all applicable protections under domestic and international law.

Recommendations the United States Supports in Part:

Recommendation 59: Legislate appropriate regulations to prevent the violations of individual privacy, constant intrusion in and control of cyberspace as well as eavesdropping of communications, by its intelligence and security organizations.

> **U.S. position**: Our Constitution and laws contain appropriate rules to protect the privacy of communications, consistent with our international human rights obligations. See also the general comments.

Recommendations 60, 137, 138, 140, 155, 166, and 217: (60) Take effective legal steps to halt human rights violations by its military forces and private security firms in Afghanistan and other States; (137) Prosecute the perpetrators of tortures, extrajudicial executions and other serious violations of human rights committed in Guantanamo, Abu Ghraib, Bagram, the NAMA and BALAD camps, and those carried out by the Joint Special Operations Command and the CIA; (138) Heed the call of the High Commissioner to launch credible independent investigations into all reliable allegations made to date of violations of international human rights law committed by American forces in Iraq, including extrajudicial killings, summary executions, and other abuses; (140) Stop the war crimes committed by its troops abroad, including the killings of innocent civilians and prosecute those who are responsible; (155) Close Guantanamo and secret centers of detention in the world, punish agents that torture, disappear and execute persons who have been arbitrarily detained, and compensate victims; (166) Take effective measures to put an end to gross human rights abuses including violence against women, committed for decades by the United States military personnel stationed in foreign bases; (217) Halt serious violations of human rights and humanitarian law including covert external operations by the CIA, carried out on the pretext of combating terrorism.

> **U.S. position**: The United States supports recommendations calling for prohibition and vigorous investigation and prosecution of any serious violations of international law, as consistent with existing U.S. law, policy, and practice. We reject those parts of these recommendations that amount to unsubstantiated accusations of ongoing serious violations by the United States. See also the general comments.

Recommendation 88: Invite United Nations Special Rapporteurs to visit and investigate Guantanamo Bay prison and United States secret prisons and to subsequently close them.

U.S. position: The United States has consistently invited United Nations Special Rapporteurs to tour the detention facility at Guantánamo, to observe detention conditions, and to observe military commission proceedings. That invitation remains. See also the general comments.

Recommendations 136, 147, 148, 156, and 157: (136) Take legal and administrative measures to address civilian killings by the US military troops during and after its invasion of Afghanistan and Iraq by investigating and bringing perpetrators to justice and remedying the victims and to close its detention facilities in foreign territories like Guantanamo, including CIA secret camps; (147) Conduct thorough and objective investigation of facts concerning use of torture against imprisoned persons in the secret prisons of United States of America and detainees of the detention centres in Bagram and Guantanamo, bring those who are responsible for these violations to justice, and undertake all necessary measures to provide redress to those whose rights were violated, including payment of necessary compensation; (148) Take measures to ensure reparation to victims of acts of torture committed under United States' control and allow access to the International Committee of the Red Cross to detention facilities under the control of the United States; (156) Expedite efforts aimed at closing the detention facility at Guantanamo Bay and ensure that all remaining detainees are tried, without delay, in accordance with the relevant international standards; Proceed with the closure of Guantanamo at the earliest possible date and bring to trial promptly in accordance with the applicable rules of international law the detainees held there or release them; (157) Quickly close down Guantanamo prison and follow the provision of the United Nations Charter and the Security Council Resolution by expatriating the terrorist suspect to their country of origin.

U.S. position: We intend to close the Guantánamo Bay detention facility. The President has closed all CIA detention facilities and has prohibited CIA operation of such facilities. We allow the International Committee of the Red Cross access to individuals detained by the United States pursuant to armed conflict. We investigate allegations of torture, and prosecute where appropriate. We cannot accept portions of these recommendations concerning reparation, redress, remedies, or compensation. Although mechanisms for remedies are available through U.S. courts, we cannot make commitments regarding their outcome. We cannot accept the part of Recommendation 136 that we close *all* detention centers; the United States maintains certain internment facilities abroad, consistent with applicable U.S. and international law. We cannot agree to the part of Recommendation 156 that we release all individuals detained pursuant to an armed conflict who are not promptly brought to trial. Regarding Recommendation 157, transfers of detainees to their home countries will only be conducted in accordance with our humane treatment policies.

Recommendation 142: Halt selective assassinations committed by contractors, and the privatization of conflicts with the use of private military companies.

U.S. position: See general comments. Our contractors are not authorized to engage in direct hostilities or offensive operations or to commit assassinations. Like U.S. government personnel, contractors may only use force consistent with our international and domestic legal obligations. We have expressed support for the International Code of Conduct for Private Security Service Providers.

Recommendation 143: End the use of military technology and weaponry that have proven to be indiscriminate and cause excessive and disproportionate damage to civilian life.

U.S. position: See general comments. In U.S. military operations, great care is taken to ensure that only legitimate objectives are targeted and that collateral damage is kept to a minimum.

Recommendation 187: Guarantee the right to privacy and stop spying on its citizens without judicial authorization.

U.S. position: See general comments. We collect information about our citizens only in accordance with U.S. law and international obligations.

5. IMMIGRATION

Recommendations the United States Supports:

Recommendation 80: Spare no efforts to constantly evaluate the enforcement of the immigration federal legislation, with a vision of promoting and protecting human rights.

Recommendation 104: Make further efforts in order to eliminate all forms of discrimination and the abuse of authority by police officers against migrants and foreigners, especially the community of Vietnamese origin people in the United States.

Recommendation 108: Prohibit and punish the use of racial profiling in all programs that enable local authorities with the enforcement of immigration legislation and provide effective and accessible recourse to remedy human rights violations occurred under these programs.

Recommendation 144: Increases its efforts to eliminate alleged brutality and use of excessive force by law enforcement officials against, inter alia, Latino and African American persons and undocumented migrants, and to ensure that relevant allegations are investigated and that perpetrators are prosecuted.

> **U.S. position**: We support this recommendation insofar as it allows for the exercise of prosecutorial discretion.

Recommendation 164, 184, and 210: (164) Ensure that detention centers for migrants and the treatment they receive meet the basic conditions and universal human rights law; (184) Adapt the detention conditions of immigrants in line with international human rights law; (210) Protect the human rights of migrants, regardless of their migratory status.

> **U.S. position**: We support these recommendations insofar as they recommend compliance with our obligations under international human rights law.

Recommendation 165: Further foster its measures in relation to migrant women and foreign adopted children that are exposed to domestic violence.

Recommendation 183: Investigate carefully each case of immigrants' incarceration.

Recommendation 185: Ensure that migrants in detention, subject to a process of expulsion are entitled to counsel, a fair trial and fully understand their rights, even in their own language.

> **U.S. position**: We support these recommendations insofar as "entitled" to counsel means that a migrant in removal proceedings in immigration court enjoys the right to counsel at his/her own expense, and "fully understand their rights" means to have been provided information in a language they understand.

Recommendation 208: Prohibit, prevent and punish the use of lethal force in carrying out immigration control activities.

U.S. position: Law enforcement and immigration officers are lawfully permitted to use deadly force under certain exceptional circumstances; e.g., self-defense or defense of another person.

Recommendation 212: Reconsider alternatives to the detention of migrants.

Recommendation 213: Ensure access of migrants to consular assistance.

> **U.S. position**: We support this recommendation understanding "consular assistance" to mean access consistent with Article 36 of the Vienna Convention on Consular Relations and similar provisions in bilateral consular agreements.

Recommendation 214: Make greater efforts to guarantee the access of migrants to basic services, regardless of their migratory status.

> **U.S. position**: We support this recommendation understanding that "basic services" refers to services such as primary education and emergency health services that are provided to migrants regardless of status.

Recommendation 220: Smarten security checks so as to take into account the frequent homonymy specific to Moslem names so as to avoid involuntary discrimination against innocent people with such names because of namesakes listed as members of terrorist groups.

Recommendation 223: Inform Foreign Missions regularly of efforts to ensure compliance with consular notification and access for foreign nationals in United States custody at all levels of law enforcement.

> **U.S. position**: We support this recommendation because it comports with the United States' general practice of widely disseminating information on its consular notification and access outreach and training efforts, including to foreign missions in the United States.

Recommendations the United States Supports in Part:

Recommendations 79 and 105: (79) Attempt to restrain any state initiative which approaches immigration issues in a repressive way towards the migrant community and that violates its rights by applying racial profiling, criminalizing undocumented immigration and violating the human and civil rights of persons; (105) Avoid the criminalization of migrants and ensure the end of police brutality, through human rights training and awareness-raising campaigns, especially to eliminate stereotypes and guarantee that the incidents of excessive use of force be investigated and the perpetrators prosecuted.

> **U.S. position**: See general comments. We will continue to both conduct human rights training and awareness campaigns and, where appropriate, bring civil or criminal actions regarding racial profiling, police brutality, and excessive use of force, and other actionable civil rights violations against immigrants. While unlawful presence in the U.S. is not a crime, and the federal government does not support state initiatives that aim to criminalize mere status, we cannot support the parts related to the "criminalization" of migrants, as certain immigration offenses are subject to criminal sanction, e.g., illegal entry.

Recommendation 82: Adopt a fair immigration policy, and cease xenophobia, racism and intolerance to ethnic, religious and migrant minorities.

> **U.S. position**: See general comments. It is consistent with our continuing efforts to improve our immigration policies and to eliminate xenophobia, racism, and intolerance in our society.

Recommendation 102: Revoke the national system to register the entry and exit of citizens of 25 countries from the Middle-East, South Asia and North Africa, and eliminate racial and other forms of profiling and stereotyping of Arabs, Muslims and South Asians as recommended by CERD.

> **U.S. position**: See general comments. Our Constitution and numerous statutes prohibit the invidious use of race or ethnicity. The registration requirements of the National Security Entry-Exit Registration System are under review at this time.

Recommendation 207: End violence and discrimination against migrants.

> **U.S. position**: See general comments.

6. LABOR AND TRAFFICKING

Recommendations the United States Supports:

Recommendation 115: Consider taking further action to better ensure gender equality at work.

> **U.S. position**: We have comprehensive laws aimed at ensuring gender equality at work, and we are taking further action through the President's Equal Pay Taskforce.

Recommendation 168: Define, prohibit and punish the trafficking of persons and child prostitution.

Recommendation 169: Insist more on measures aiming to combat the demand and provide information and services to victims of trafficking.

Recommendation 192: Recognize the right to association as established by ILO, for migrant, agricultural workers and domestic workers.

> **U.S. position**: We support the 1998 ILO Declaration on Fundamental Principles and Rights at Work, which reaffirms the commitment of all ILO Member States to respect, promote, and realize principles concerning fundamental rights in four categories including freedom of association and collective bargaining. Although not a party to ILO conventions 87 and 98 on those topics, we have robust laws addressing their fundamental principles.

Recommendation 193: Prevent slavery of agriculture workers, in particular children and women.

Recommendations the United States Supports in Part:

Recommendation 81: Take the necessary measures in favor of the right to work and fair conditions of work so that workers belonging to minorities, in particular women and undocumented migrant workers, do not become victims of discriminatory treatment and abuse in the work place and enjoy the full protection of the labor legislation, regardless of their migratory status.

> **U.S. position**: Members of minority groups enjoy important anti-discrimination and labor protections. While labor laws apply to undocumented migrant workers, such individuals may not be entitled to certain types of remedies.

7. ECONOMIC, SOCIAL, AND CULTURAL RIGHTS AND MEASURES

Recommendations the United States Supports:

Recommendation 109: Promote equal socio-economic as well as educational opportunities for all both in law and in fact, regardless of their ethnicity, race, religion, national origin, gender or disability.

Recommendation 113: That further measures be taken in the areas of economic and social rights for women and minorities, including providing equal access to decent work and reducing the number of homeless people.

Recommendation 195: Ensure the realization of the rights to food and health of all who live in its territory.

> **U.S. position**: We are a non-party to the International Covenant on Economic, Social and Cultural Rights, and accordingly we understand the references to rights to food and health as references to rights in other human rights instruments that we have accepted. We also understand that these rights are to be realized progressively.

Recommendation 196: Expand its social protection coverage.

> **U.S. position**: The U.S. government seeks to improve the safety net that our country provides for the less fortunate.

Recommendation 197: Continue its efforts in the domain of access to housing, vital for the realization of several other rights, in order to meet the needs for adequate housing at an affordable price for all segments of the American society.

Recommendation 226: Persevere in the strengthening of its aid to development, considered as fundamental, in particular the assistance and relief in case of natural disasters.

8. THE ENVIRONMENT

Recommendations the United States Supports in Part:

Recommendations 51, 221, and 222: (51) Comply with its international obligations for the effective mitigation of greenhouse gas emissions, because of their impact in climate change; (221) Take positive steps in regard to climate change, by assuming the responsibilities arising from capitalism that have generated major natural disasters particularly in the most impoverished countries; (222) Implement the necessary reforms to reduce their greenhouse gas emissions and cooperate with the international community to mitigate threats against human rights resulting from climate change.

> **U.S. position**: See general comments. We disagree with premises embedded in these recommendations, but agree with their essential objectives (reduce greenhouse gas emissions and cooperate internationally).

9. DOMESTIC IMPLEMENTATION OF HUMAN RIGHTS

Recommendations the United States Supports:

Recommendation 65: Review its laws at the Federal and State levels with a view to bringing them in line with its international human rights obligations.

> **U.S. position**: We regularly engage in such reviews of our laws in light of our human rights obligations, including through the enforcement of our Federal civil rights laws and implementation of our domestic civil rights programs, litigation and judicial review, our reports to UN human rights treaty bodies, engagement with UN Special Procedures, and active discussions with civil society. Although the Federal government does not consistently or systematically review State laws, our civil rights mechanisms allow for review of State laws, as appropriate.

Recommendation 74: That a human rights institution at the federal level be considered in order to ensure implementation of human rights in all states.

> **U.S. position**: There are Federal and State institutions to monitor human rights; we are considering whether this network of protection is in need of improvement.

Recommendation 87: Incorporate human rights training and education strategies in their public policies.

> **U.S. position**: Programs at the Federal and State levels provide training on human rights, particularly on issues related to civil rights and non-discrimination; we are continuing to explore ways to strengthen such programs.

Recommendation 225: Continue consultations with non-governmental organizations and civil society in the follow up.

Recommendations the United States Supports in Part:

Recommendation 227: That the model legal framework expressed by the Leahy Laws be applied with respect to all countries receiving US's security assistance, and that the human rights records of all units receiving such assistance be documented, evaluated, made available and followed up upon in cases of abuse.

> **U.S. position**: This recommendation enjoys our support except for the last part regarding making our decision-making publicly available. We apply the Leahy laws (which impose human rights-related restrictions on assistance to foreign security forces) to all countries receiving U.S. security assistance, and we respond appropriately in cases of abuse. However, to do so, we consider information from all sources, including classified sources, and cannot make our decision-making public.

10. TREATIES AND INTERNATIONAL HUMAN RIGHTS MECHANISMS

Recommendations the United States Supports:

Recommendations 10, 11, 13, 14, 20, 21, 22, 26, 28, 30, 33, 34, 35, 39, 43, 47, 48, 49, and 93: (10) Consider ratifying ICESCR, CEDAW and CRC at the earliest; (11) Consider undertaking necessary steps leading to ratification of the parent/umbrella United Nations Convention on the Rights of the Child and CEDAW respectively; (13) Proceed with ratifying the CRPD and CRC; (14) Ratify, and ensure implementation into domestic law of CEDAW and CRC; (20) Consider ratifying the treaties to which it is not a party, including the CEDAW, CRC, ICESCR, and CRPD; (21) Consider ratifying CEDAW, the Convention on the Rights of the Child, and the Convention on the Rights of Persons with Disabilities;

(22) Consider prioritizing acquiescence to the Convention of the Rights of the Child, CEDAW, the ILO Convention No. 111 on Discrimination in Respect of Employment and Occupation so as to further strengthen its national framework for human rights, but also to assist in achieving their universality; (26) Consider ratifying ILO Convention 100 on equal remuneration for men and women for work of equal value, and ILO Convention 111 on discrimination in employment and occupation; (28) Consider ratifying the Rome Statute of the International Criminal Court and the Additional Protocols I and II of the Geneva Conventions; (30) Consider signing the International Convention on the Protection of the Rights of All Migrant Workers and Members of Their Families; (33) Swiftly ratify CEDAW; Ratify CEDAW; Become a party to CEDAW; (34) Ratify the Convention on the Rights of the Child; Become a party to the Convention on the Rights of the Child; (35) Ratify the Convention on the Rights of Persons with Disabilities as a matter of priority; Become a party to the Convention on the Rights of Persons with Disabilities; (39) Examine the possibility of ratifying the core human rights treaties to which the country is not yet a party and raising its reservations on those which it has ratified; (43) Consider the signing, ratification or accession, as corresponds, of the main international and Inter-American human rights instruments, especially the Convention on the Rights of the Child; (47) Consider lifting reservations to a number of ICCPR articles; (48) Take the necessary measures to consider lifting the United States reservation to article 5, paragraph 6 of the International Covenant on Civil and Political Rights that bans the imposition of the death penalty for crimes committed by persons under 18; (49) Consider the withdrawal of all reservations and declarations that undermine the objective and spirit of the human rights instruments, in particular reservation to article 6 paragraph 5 of the International Covenant on Civil and Political Rights that bans the imposition of the death penalty to those who committed a crime when they were minors;(93) Consider extending a standing invitation to special procedures.

U.S. position: We support the recommendations asking us to ratify the Convention on the Elimination of All Forms of Discrimination against Women, the Convention on the Rights of Persons with Disabilities, and ILO Convention 111. We also support the recommendations that we ratify the Convention on the Rights of the Child, as we support its goals and intend to review how we could move toward its ratification. We also support recommendations urging deliberative treaty actions, such as that we "consider ratifying" them.

Recommendation 54: Take appropriate action to resolve the obstacles that prevent the full implementation of the *Avena* Judgment of the International Court of Justice and, until this occurs, avoid the execution of the individuals covered in said judgment.

U.S. position: This recommendation is consistent with the longstanding U.S. policy of supporting the International Court of Justice and taking appropriate action to comply with judgments of the Court. The United States intends to continue to make best efforts to ensure compliance with the *Avena* judgment.

Recommendations the United States Supports in Part:

Recommendations 1-9, 15-19, 23, 24, 25, 27, 37, 38, 40, 41, and 42: (1) Ratify without reservations the following conventions and protocols: CEDAW; the ICESCR; the Convention on the Rights of the Child; the Convention on the Rights of Persons with Disabilities; the International Convention on the Protection of the Rights of All Migrant Workers and Members of Their Families; the International Convention for the Protection of All Persons from Enforced Disappearance; the Statute of the International Criminal Court; those of the ILO; the United Nations Declaration on Indigenous Peoples, and all those from the Inter-American Human Rights System; (2) Continue the process to ratify CEDAW and adhere to the other human rights fundamental instruments, such as the Statute of Rome of the International Criminal Court, the Convention on the Rights of the Child, the Optional Protocol to the Convention against Torture and the International Convention for the Protection of all Persons against Enforced Disappearance; (3) Ratify, until the next universal periodic review, ICESCR, the Convention on the Rights of the Child, Protocols I and II of the Geneva Conventions of 12 August 1949, ILO Conventions no. 87 (on freedom of association) and no. 98 (on the right to collective bargaining) as well as withdraw the reservation made to article 4 of the International Convention on the Elimination of Racial Discrimination; (4) Ratify ICESCR and its Optional Protocol; the first Optional Protocol to the International Covenant of Civil and Political Rights, CEDAW, the Convention on the Rights of the Child, the Optional Protocol to the Convention against Torture, the Convention on the Rights of Persons with Disabilities, the Convention for the Protection of All Persons from Enforced Disappearance; (5) Continue its efforts to realise universal human rights by a) ratifying CEDAW; b) becoming a party to the United Nations Convention on the Rights of the Child; c) acceding to ICESCR; d) ratifying the United Nations Convention on the Rights of Persons with Disabilities; (6) Ratify the core human rights treaties, particularly the CRC, ICESCR, CEDAW and its Optional Protocol, the OP-CAT and the CMW and the CRPD with its Optional Protocol; (7) Ratify the ICESCR, CEDAW and the Convention of the Rights of the Child at an early stage together with other important human rights conventions; (8) Ratify CEDAW, ICESCR, and CRC in token of its commitment to their implementation worldwide, as well as become party to other international human rights conventions as referred to in the OHCHR report; (9) Ratify all core international instruments on human rights, in particular ICESCR, CEDAW, the Convention on the Rights of the Child; (15) Ratify the Convention on the Rights of the Child and the International Convention on the Protection of the Rights of All Migrant Workers and Members of Their Families; (16) Endeavour to ratify international instruments that USA is not party, in particular among others the CRC, OP-CAT; CEDAW; and Rome Statute of the International Criminal Court; (17) Ratify ICESCR, CEDAW, the Convention on the Rights of the Child; the Convention on the Rights of Persons with Disabilities and other core human rights treaties as soon as possible; (18) Ratify additional human rights treaties such as the ICESCR; the Convention of the Rights of the Child; the International Convention for the Protection of All Persons from Enforced Disappearances and the Convention on Rights of Persons with Disabilities in order to further strengthen their support to the United Nations Human Rights mechanisms; (19) Ratify the pending core international human rights instruments, in particular CRC, ICESCR, and its OP, CEDAW and its OP as well as CRPD, and others, and ensure their due translation into the domestic legislation and review existing ratifications with a view to withdraw all reservations and declarations; (23) Proceed with the ratification of Additional Protocols I and II of the Geneva Conventions of 1949, of the Convention on the Rights of the Child, of CEDAW as well as the Optional Protocol to the Convention against Torture; (24) Ratify at its earliest opportunity other core human rights instruments, particularly, those to which it is already a signatory, namely CEDAW, Convention on the Rights of the Child, ICESCR, and the Convention on the Rights of Persons with Disabilities; (25) Ratify the ICESCR, CEDAW, CRC the CRPD, the Additional Protocol I and II (1977), to the Geneva Conventions, the ICC Statute, as well as the 1st and 2nd Protocol to the Hague Convention 1954; (27) Accede to ICESCR, the CRC and ILO convention No. 111. (37) Ratify the 12 international human rights instruments to which it is not a party; (38) Implement a program of ratification of all international human rights instruments, and then proceed to the incorporation of these in its internal legal system; (40) Accede to international human rights instruments which is not yet acceded to; (41) Continue the process to ratify and implement into domestic law the several international human rights instruments that still wait for this formal acceptance; (42) Accede to the universal core treaties on human rights and those of inter-American system, in particular the recognition of the jurisdiction of the Inter-American Court on Human Rights.

U.S. position: We support the parts of these recommendations asking us to ratify those treaties, identified above, of which the Administration is most committed to pursuing ratification. We cannot support the other portions. Nor can we support "without reservations" in Recommendation 1.

Recommendation 29: Ratify the Convention on the Protection of the Rights of All Migrant Workers and Members of their Families and observe international standards in this regard.

U.S. position: We support the second part ("observe international standards ..."), understanding such standards to mean applicable international human rights law.

Recommendations 44 and 45: (44) Withdraw all reservations and declarations on the international instruments to which it is a party that undermine its obligations or the purpose of the treaty; (45) Withdraw reservations, denunciations, and interpretations of the Covenant on Civil and Political Rights; the International Convention on the Elimination of All Forms of Racial Discrimination and the Convention against Torture, that undermine their compliance, and accept their individual procedures.

U.S. position: See general comments. We do not believe that any reservations, understandings, and declarations accompanying our ratification of international instruments undermine our obligations, or the treaty's object or purpose. We cannot support the part of Recommendation 45 regarding individual procedures.

Recommendation 52: Ensure the implementation of its obligations under international humanitarian law vis-à-vis Palestinian people.

U.S. position: See general comments. The U.S. government complies with its international humanitarian law obligations, but we note that international humanitarian law governs conduct in the context of armed conflict, and cannot accept this recommendation's implication that we are in an armed conflict with the Palestinian people.

Annex V: U.S. Treaty Reports 2013-2014

Optional Protocols to the Convention on the Rights of the Child
Submitted January 25, 2010
Presented January 16, 2013

International Covenant on Civil and Political Rights (ICCPR)
Submitted December 30, 2011
Presented March 13-14, 2014

Convention on the Elimination of Racial Discrimination (CERD)
Submitted June 12, 2013
Presented August 13-14, 2014

Convention Against Torture and Other Cruel, Inhuman or Degrading Treatment or Punishment (CAT)
Submitted August 12, 2013
Presented November 12-13, 2014

www.ingramcontent.com/pod-product-compliance
Lightning Source LLC
Chambersburg PA
CBHW081125280526
45787CB00007B/2981